HOW TO MAKE
PAPER CUTS AND
SILHOUETTES

HOW TO MAKE PAPER CUTS AND SILHOUETTES

Devised and drawn

by

ROSALIE BROWN

JADE PUBLISHERS
HASLEMERE

Jade Publishers
15 Stoatley Rise
Haslemere
Surrey GU27 1AF

First published 1983
Revised edition 1990
© Copyright Rosalie Brown 1983, 1990
Cover design © Copyright Jade Publishers

Cover illustrations by Alma Spriggs
Cover design by Samantha Edwards

Typeset by 'Keyword', Aldbury, Herts, and
printed and bound by Hillman Printers Ltd, Frome

British Library Cataloguing in Publication Data
Brown, Rosalie, *1912–*
How to make paper cuts and silhouettes
1. Paper. Cutting & folding
I. Title
736.98

ISBN 0–903461–34–X

CONTENTS

(Continued)

Silhouettes

INTRODUCTION

Almost all you need to make delightful cutouts and silhouettes are paper and sharp scissors – and your own nimble fingers, of course.

As well as having hours of fun making different shapes and figures, you can make your own gifts for family or friends and lovely decorations for the home at the same time!

Starting with the simpler designs, move on through the pages of the book, tackling the trickier figures as you become more skilful. The best results are gained when you work carefully and patiently, taking time to read the instructions through before you make the first snip of the scissors.

Spread newspaper or other protective coating over the surface you're going to be working on. It's a good idea to keep a damp cloth handy for wiping up spills or sticky fingers, and a rubbish bin to dispose of cut-out scraps.

ROSALIE BROWN

MATERIALS REQUIRED

Black Indian ink or poster paint, and brush

Blotting paper or clean scrap paper

Board for cutting on – a chopping board, hardboard or thick, smooth cardboard (not the corrugated kind)

Board for mounting cutouts – hardboard or thick, smooth cardboard

Clear varnishing lacquer

Craft knife with a sharp point

Drawing compass

Drawing pins or blue tack

Hole puncher

Light fabric

Newspaper to spread for a working surface

Old magazines, comics, catalogues, newspapers and other illustrated publications to cut up

Paper – you will need black, white and coloured paper in different thicknesses
  a. stiff paper or card for mounting cutouts
  b. gummed paper
  c. thin paper to fold and cut
  d. black poster paper (not too thick, to allow for neat cutting). This is available from art shops and larger stationers. In some shops you may be able to buy sheets of black paper with one side already gummed – these are handy and save the trouble of using paste. If you cannot get the black paper at all, use white paper instead and follow the instructions for using black Indian ink or paint on pages 52 and 54.

Paste and brush	Steel ruler
Pinking shears	Sticky tape
Ruler	Tracing paper
Rubber	White ink or paint, and brush
Small, sharp scissors	White pencil, crayon or chalk
Soft lead pencil	White sticky labels

PAPER CUTS

NAMEPLATES

Materials: a. Paper, any colour
              b. Pencil
              c. Scissors

In the past, craftsmen fashioning brass or other metal fittings for their beautifully made wares used this method of folding and cutting out paper shapes to make the stencils they needed.

1.   Fold a square or rectangle of paper in half from left to right.

2.   Draw the outline you want on to the paper with pencil and cut it out through both thicknesses of paper.

3.   Open the paper out to its full size (see figs. a, b, c).

Taking the method described one step further, you can make more elaborate shapes.

1.   Fold a rectangle of paper in half from left to right, and then fold it in half again from top to bottom. This will give you a small rectangle with 4 thicknesses of paper.

2.   Draw the outline on to the paper with pencil and cut it out through all thicknesses of paper.

3.   Open the paper out to its full size (see fig. d).

These simple shapes have been copied from old brasswork, and were originally used as ornamental nameplates for inscriptions on boxes.

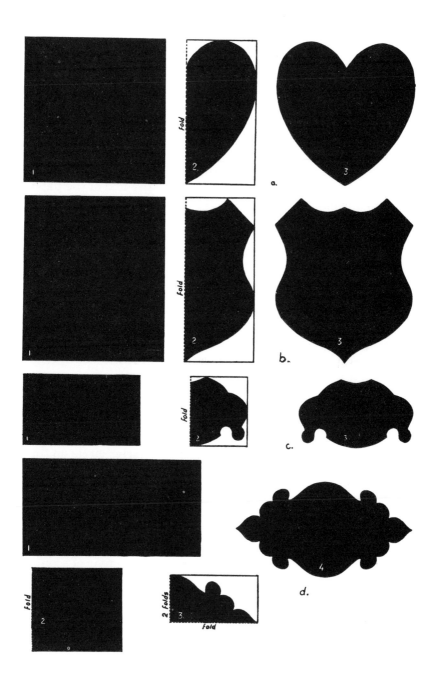

a.

b.

c.

d.

11

DECORATIVE KEYHOLES

Materials: a. Paper, any colour
                b. Pencil
                c. Scissors

These shapes were first used for decorative metal keyhole surrounds, or escutcheons.

1.   Fold a rectangle of paper in half from left to right. Draw the outline on to the paper and cut it out through the double thickness. Notice the cut to be made on the fold of the paper – when opened out again a hole is left in the centre of the shape (see fig. a).

2.   To make a keyhole-shaped hole in the centre, fold a rectangle of paper in half from left to right and cut a half keyhole halfway down the fold. Then, fold the paper in half again from top to bottom. Draw on the outside outline and cut that out (see fig. b).

3.   For fancier perforations, fold the paper twice, first from left to right and then from top to bottom. Cut out the outline through all 4 thicknesses of paper (see fig. c).

4.   A variation on the same idea is to cut the keyhole shape out first through a double thickness of paper folded once from left to right. Fold the paper again from top to bottom and cut around the outline. By cutting a small quarter circle on the edge of the lower fold, circular notches in the sides are formed (see fig. d).

5.   Being more adventurous still, cut the keyhole shape through a double thickness of paper folded once from left to right. Fold in half again from top to bottom, then draw and cut out the outline. Using the point of a small, sharp pair of scissors, pierce all 4 thicknesses of paper to cut out extra shapes inside the larger outline (see fig. e).

a.

b.

c.

d.

e.

SURROUNDS FOR HANDLES

Materials: a. Paper, any colour
                     b. Pencil
                     c. Scissors

Surrounds for drawer and cupboard handles give a pleasing effect and can be made from these shapes:

1.   Fold a rectangle of paper in half once from left to right. Draw on the outline and cut out through both thicknesses of paper (see fig. a).

2.   Use the point of a small, sharp pair of scissors to pierce the double thickness of paper and cut out extra small shapes within the overall outline (see fig. b).

3.   To make a string of identical shapes for a border, use a much longer strip of paper than usual. Fold it backwards and forwards in a fan-like manner to the size required. Notice there are folds on both the left and right sides of the paper now. Draw on the outline and cut it out. Be sure the outline touches against both the left and right folds, or the paper will fall apart when opened out to its full length again. Pierce the smaller holes with the point of sharp scissors and cut them out through all the thicknesses of paper. Unless you are using thin paper, you may find it difficult to cut through more than a few thicknesses of paper at once (see figs. c and d).

a.

b.

c and d.

long strip folded like this →

c.

d.

15

CENTRE AND CORNER PIECES

Materials: a. Paper, any colour
                 b. Pencil
                 c. Scissors

A cut-out centre piece and corner pieces add an attractive feature to a games box or any other kind of box you choose to decorate.

1.   Cut out a circle from plain or coloured paper. You may first wish to trace around the rim of a plate or other round object, or use a drawing compass to get the shape right.

2.   Fold the circle in half once to form a semi-circle, then in half again, and once again, so that the shape resembles only a segment of a circle. There will now be 8 thicknesses of paper, so unless you are using thin paper it may not be possible to cut crisp, clear outlines easily.

3.   Draw the outline on and cut out. Remember that the outline must touch against both left and right folds of the segment. To cut the small, inner shape, pierce all thicknesses of paper with the point of a small, sharp pair of scissors and carefully cut away the shape.

4.   Opened out again to its full size, the centre piece is complete (fig. a).

5.   For the corner pieces, use paper cut into quarter circles. Fold each one in half only once this time.

6.   Draw the outline on to the paper and cut out in the same way as for the centre piece. Once again, make sure the outline touches both sides of the segment (fig. b).

7.   To have the centre and corner pieces of matching design, use the same outline for each one.

CENTRE PIECE

fold

a.

1

2

2 folds

3

fold

a.

3 folds

4

fold.

a.

3 folds

5

fold.

b.

6.

a.

b.

1.

quarter circle

fold

2

2 edges

b.

CORNER PIECE

fold

3

2 edges

b.

4

17

DOILIES AND MATS

Materials: a. Paper, any colour
               b. Pencil
               c. Scissors

The first cutouts children make are often doilies or mats cut from tissue or thin paper, like these:

1.   Fold a square of thin plain or coloured paper in half and in half again to form a smaller square with 4 thicknesses of paper.

2.   Cut notches in each side of the square. Opened out again, this makes a pretty pattern (see fig. a). Use the same method with a circle of paper to make a round doily (see fig. b).

As you become more skilful and confident with the scissors, you can fold the paper even smaller after making the first cuts, and make extra cuts on the new folds.

1.   Fold a square of paper in half, then in half again to form a smaller square. Fold this in half once more to make an oblong with 8 thicknesses of paper. Cut notches on each of the 4 sides, through all the thicknesses of paper, and open out (see fig. c).

2.   Alternatively, fold the square in half and in half again. Fold this smaller square from corner to corner, making a triangle shape. Cut notches through all the thicknesses in each of the 3 sides. Opened out, this gives a quite different pattern (see fig. d).

3.   Using a circle instead, fold it in half once, twice and 3 times, then cut notches around the 3 edges and open out (see fig. e).

From these simple beginnings, you can progress to more complicated designs, experimenting and trying out your own ideas as you go.

DIFFERENT MOTIFS

Materials: a. Paper, any colour
                   b. Pencil
                   c. Scissors

By folding squares of paper in different ways, the same simple motif can have very different results.

1. Fold a square of paper in half from corner to corner into a triangle shape. Cut a scroll design on the fold and notches around the other 2 edges (see fig. a).

2. Fold a square of paper in half to form a triangle, then fold once again to give a small triangle with 4 thicknesses of paper. Cut the same scroll design used for the previous example on the single fold and cut notches on the other 2 edges (see fig. b).

3. This time, fold a square 3 times so there are 8 thicknesses of paper. Cut the same scroll design on the single, thick fold and notches on the other 2 sides (see fig. c).

4. As before, fold a square 3 times into a small triangle. Cut the scroll into the single, thick fold, but from the opposite direction. Cut notches on the other 2 edges (see fig. d).

It is interesting to see how the final effect can vary, using the same design in each case but folding the paper differently and cutting into different edges of the shape.

CIRCULAR SHAPES

Materials: a. Paper, any colour
              b. Pencil
              c. Scissors

Just as folding a square of paper in different ways varies the cut-out effect dramatically, the same can be achieved by using circular shapes.

1.   Fold a circle of paper in half once to make a semi-circle. Cut the scroll motif into the folded edge and notches around the curved edge (see fig. a).

2.   Fold a circle of paper in half twice, giving 4 thicknesses of paper. Cut the scroll motif into the edge with 2 folds and notches around the other 2 sides (see fig. b).

3.   Fold the paper circle in half twice, as above, but this time cut the design into the side with one single fold, and notches elsewhere (see fig. c).

4.   Fold a circle of paper in half 3 times, to make 8 thicknesses of paper. Cut the design into the edge with 3 folds, from the point of the shape towards the curved edge (see fig. d).

5.   Again, fold a paper circle 3 times and cut the design on the 3-fold edge, as above, but this time cut the design in from the opposite direction, from near the curved edge towards the point of the shape (see fig. e).

Experiment with this theme – try cutting the design into the single fold rather than the double or triple fold, and vice versa, or cut the design in different directions, towards the point and away from it.

fold

a.

fold

a.

one fold

b.

2 folds

one fold

b.

2 folds

one fold

c.

2 folds

one fold

c.

2 folds

one fold

d.

3 folds

one fold

d.

3 folds

e.

3 folds

one fold

one fold

3 folds

23

GUMMED CUTOUTS

Materials: a. Gummed black or coloured paper
             b. Hole puncher
             c. Paper for cutting
             d. Pencil
             e. Small, sharp scissors
             f. White sticky labels

1.   Using a square or rectangle of gummed paper with a white back or a gummed label, fold in half with the white sticky side facing outward. Draw a scroll motif on to the paper (figs. a) and cut out the design (figs. b). The black colour in the illustrations shows the areas that have been cut away.

2.   Unfold the shape and stick down on a coloured backing sheet to highlight the design (figs. c). Here, black represents the designs.

The results can be made more stunning by making fancier cuts (see figs. d, e, f). Use a hole puncher to make small circles.

BRASSWORK DESIGNS

Materials: a. Coloured backing paper
              b. Paper for cutting, any colour
              c. Paste and brush
              d. Pencil
              e. Scissors

These designs, copied from old brasswork, are further ideas for eye-catching cutouts.

1. Fold a long strip of paper in half lengthwise. Draw and cut out a pattern. Open the strip out and mount on a coloured background (see fig. a). Notice this design is cut with a border around the edge.

2. Fold a long strip of paper in half lengthwise, then in half again from top to bottom. Draw and cut out a pattern. Open the paper out and stick down on a coloured backing sheet (see fig. b). This design has also been cut with a border.

3. Fold a square of paper in half lengthwise and again from top to bottom. Then fold from corner to corner to make a triangle shape of 8 paper thicknesses. Draw and cut out a pattern. Open the square out and mount on a coloured background (see fig. c).

4. Fold a rectangle of paper in half lengthwise. Fold in half again from top to bottom, forming a small rectangle. Rule a line from the bottom left corner to the top right corner. Cut along this line and discard the loose triangles. Work with the triangle which has one edge on a single fold and another with 2 folds. Draw a design along the side with loose edges and cut out. Open the shape out and paste down on a coloured backing sheet (see fig. d).

5. Alternatively, use the above methods but cut the design along all 3 sides and in the centre of the triangle, using the point of small, sharp scissors to pierce the thicknesses (see fig. e).

a.

fold

2 folds

one fold

b.

c.

folded
smaller
square

edges

folds

d.

this
half is
cut off

edges

two folds

one fold

edges

two folds

one fold

e.

edges

27

OCTAGONS

Materials: a. Drawing compass, if available
                b. Paper, any colour
                c. Pencil
                d. Ruler
                e. Scissors

Making an 8-sided shape, or octagon, is quite simple, following these steps:

1.   Use a drawing compass to outline a circle on paper, or trace around the rim of a plate or other round object. Cut out the shape.

2.   Fold the circle in half 3 times, so there are 8 thicknesses of paper. Crease each fold firmly. Opened out again, the fold marks divide the circle into 8 equal sections (see fig. a).

3.   Refold the circle 3 times. Draw and cut out a design. Or fold the shape in half a fourth time and then draw and cut out a design. Remember that this extra folding may be too thick to cut through unless you use thin paper and sharp scissors.

4.   If you want straight edges to your octagon rather than curved, simply rule a line from fold to fold on the circle's outer edge and cut the edge away (see fig. b).

STARS

Materials: a. Paper, any colour
               b. Pencil
               c. Ruler
               d. Scissors

To fold and cut a pentagon, or star with 5 points, follow these steps and the diagrams opposite:

1. Fold a square of paper in half. Measure and make a mark (X) in the exact centre of the fold between A and B as shown on fig. 1.

2. Find the centre point on the left edge between A and C and mark it (Y). Find and mark the halfway point between Y and C (Z).

3. Bend corner A over to make a fold from X to Z. Crease the fold firmly and open out again.

4. Bring corner B down to meet this fold line and crease the new fold well.

5. Bend the new corner E over to join B and crease again.

6. Fold corner A backwards along the same X–Z line to meet corner F on the other side.

7. Cut straight across from E to the X–F fold. The sharpness of the points of the star depends on the angle you cut from E, as you will find with practice.

8. Unfold the shape now, and there you have a star.

9. Refold the shape as it was, draw and cut a pattern into the edges and open out again.

If you want to draw a pentagon shape, fold and cut out a star as described. Place the star on paper and make a mark at the tip of each point of the star on the paper. Remove the star and rule lines to join up the marks.

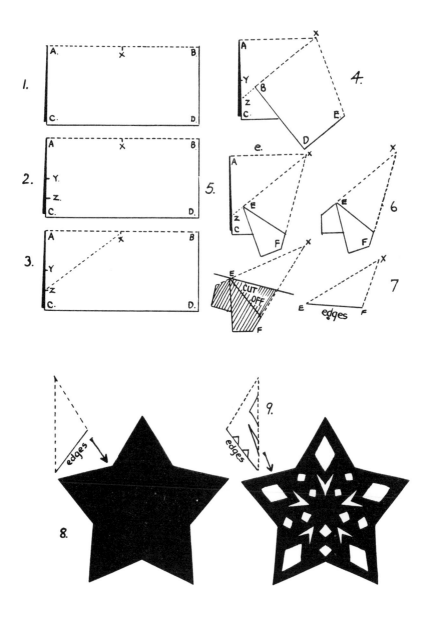

1.

2.

3.

4.

5.

6.

7

8.

9.

31

SNOWFLAKES

Materials: a. Black backing paper or card   d. Paste and brush
                        b. Drawing compass, if available e. Pencil
                        c. Paper for cutting –   f. Ruler
                            white looks best   g. Scissors

1. Using a drawing compass, draw a circle (see fig. a).
2. Without altering the compass, make a mark on the edge of the circle. Place the needle of the compass on the mark and with the pencil make another mark where it touches the circle further along. Repeat this right around the circle until you meet the first mark again (see fig. b).
3. Rule lines through the circle from each pencil mark to the one directly opposite (see fig. c).
4. At the edge of the circle, rule straight lines from pencil mark to pencil mark. Cut out this shape to give a hexagon (see fig. d).

If you do not have a drawing compass, make the hexagon in this way:

1. Using a plate or other round object, trace a circle on to paper and cut out (see fig. a).
2. Fold the circle carefully in half, making sure the curved edges meet exactly. Crease the fold firmly (see fig. e).
3. Fold the shape in half again and crease the new fold well (see fig. f).
4. Open the circle out. Where the two crease marks cross one another is the centre point (see fig. g).
5. Take a strip of paper (or a ruler) and measure from the centre point of the circle to the edge. Mark the paper strip where it touches the centre and where it crosses the outside edge (see fig. h).
6. Beginning from one of the fold marks on the circle, measure around the outside with the paper strip, taking care to have the 2 marks on the strip touching the circle's edge. Make a dot or small mark on the circle where they touch. Do this all around the edge until you meet the starting point again (see fig. i).
7. Rule straight lines from each mark to the one directly opposite it (see fig. c).

Now, fold the circle in half along one of the ruled lines and crease it well (see fig. j). Without opening the circle out, fold along another of the drawn lines (see fig. k) and finally along the remaining line (see fig. l). The folds should lie together evenly. Crease firmly.

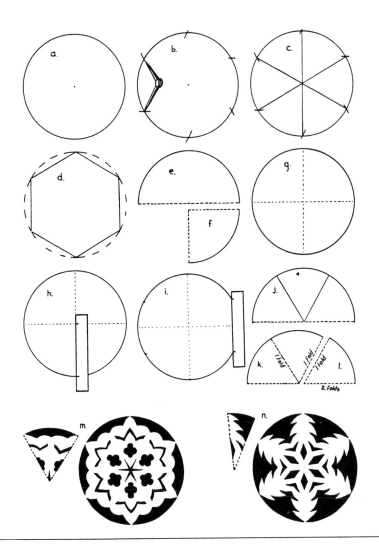

Make cuts into the folded shape with your scissors and use a hole punch to make small circles (see fig. m). Or, fold the shape in half again and cut out the design (see fig. n). Unless your paper is quite thin and your scissors sharp, this will not work successfully. Mount the snowflake cutouts on a black background to show up the designs. With practice, more complicated and elaborate patterns can be made.

GREETINGS CARDS

Materials: a. Coloured backing paper or card
            b. Paper for cutting, any colour
            c. Paste and brush
            d. Pencil
            e. Scissors

You can make your own attractive greetings cards for all occasions using the methods described on the previous pages. Here are some further ideas.

1. The Christmas tree (see fig. a) can be as simple or elaborate as you please. Fold a square of paper in half once, draw on the design, leaving a small border around the edges, and cut out. Or, fold the paper a second time, from top to bottom. Draw on the design, leaving a small border around the edges, and cut out. Folded 3 times instead, the result is even more intricate.

2. Fold a square of paper in half just once. Cut a heart-shaped outline first, then draw and cut out your design (see fig. b).

3. Fold a square of paper in half once, and then again from left to right, giving a long, narrow shape. Draw and cut out your design, leaving a small border around the edges (see fig. c).

    The black area in figs. a, b and c indicate the part to be cut away.

4. The four emblems of the United Kingdom – These striking figures are cut from a square of paper folded in half once (see fig. d).

Mount the cutout on a coloured sheet of card folded in half and write your message inside. The receiver of your 'home-made' card will be delighted with its originality and the thought that went into its making.

USING FIGURES

Figures of people, animals, birds or insects can be used for any of the styles of folding and cutting described in earlier pages. The figures shown opposite are cut from paper folded in half once.

Small details like the rabbit's whiskers may be added in ink, and circles such as those on the butterfly's wings can be made with a hole puncher.

For grass, fur or other ruffled edges like those on the giraffe cutout, first cut out the shape as you would usually. Then make a series of tiny cuts from the edge of the outline down, in one direction. Cut back in the other direction and small pieces will drop away, leaving the grass or other effect you seek. You may wish to practise doing this on a scrap of paper if you are unsure.

If you cannot draw figures, make a tracing around the outline of a figure in a magazine, card or other source you'd like to use. Choose a profile or side view rather than a full face. Rub the tracing off on to the back of a piece of folded paper, taking care that some part of the figure touches against the folded edge. Cut out carefully, cutting away the small pieces first and the larger areas last. You may find it easiest to cut from the edges towards the fold rather than the other way.

When you are mounting these on card or other stiff backing sheets, place the bottom edge of the figure down first. When it is in position, press it firmly but not roughly with your fingers, then carefully smooth the rest of the figure down. Place blotting paper or clear scrap paper over the top and press down to absorb any dampness.

ODD SHAPES

Materials: a. Paper, any colour
                b. Pencil
                c. Scissors

The choice of shapes from which to make cutouts is as wide as you like. Use your imagination freely and experiment. It is possible to use up offcuts of paper with the ideas shown here.

1. Using an odd, boat-shaped piece of paper, fold twice to make a triangle. Cut a design into all 3 sides and in the centre by piercing the 4 thicknesses of paper with the point of sharp scissors (see fig. a).

2. Fold an oval shape in half from left to right and again from top to bottom. Cut the pattern into all sides, and in the centre using the point of sharp scissors to pierce the paper (see fig. b).

3. Fold a diamond shape in half twice and cut a design as described above (see fig. c).

4. Using an offcut from the makings of an earlier, different shape, fold the paper in half once from left to right and cut out a pattern (see fig. d).

first folding

Fig a

second fold

open out the triangle to cut round the edges →

first folding

Fig. b.

second folding

Fig c.

first folding

second folding

1.

2.

Fig d.

Six patterns using off-cuts from other cut shapes

3.

4.

5.

6.

BORDERS

Materials: a. Ruler
                b. Paper, any colour
                c. Pencil
                d. Scissors

1.   For a border strip, fold a long strip of paper backwards and forwards equally in a zigzag, concertina fashion. The border shown (fig. A) has been folded 8 times and the designs drawn and cut out. The figures at the top show other designs.

2.   To make a border with a fancy corner (fig. B):
    a. Cut the basic shape of paper out with an extra notch on the inside corner.
    b. Bring the outside corner up to meet the inside notch, and fold.
    c. Bend the vertical strip over to lie neatly along the horizontal strip. The new fold should run through the centre of the corner top (x).
    d. Fold the doubled strip over and over as far as x.
       To make a neat job of this folding, measure the strip first and divide it into equal parts.
    e. To make the first cut as shown, bend the corner piece x backwards against the folded strip. On the new fold made, cut out a notch then bring the corner piece x back to its previous position.
    f. Make the remaining cuts on the folded strip and corner piece, and open out.

3.   To make a border with a plain corner (fig. C):
    a. Cut out the basic shape of paper without an extra notch on the inside corner. Fold the vertical strip down on to the horizontal strip neatly.
    b. Fold the doubled strip backwards and forwards in equal portions in a zigzag manner right up to line xx.
    c. Bend the corner over along line xx to make the first cuts, then unfold to its previous position and continue cutting the rest of the pattern. When finished, open out.

x   Y

z

a.

x

Y on z

1 fold

c.

1 fold, 1 edge

x on Y and Z

1 fold

1 fold

1 fold, 1 edge.

edges

2 folds

b.

2 folds

1 fold

c.

C.

d.

a.

b.

c.

a.

b.

c.

B.

d.

e.

f.

A.

41

ADDING COLOURS

Materials: a. Board for mounting pictures –
               hardboard to thick, smooth cardboard
           b. Hole puncher
           c. Ink or paint, and brush
           d. Paper – white, black and coloured
           e. Pencil
           f. Pinking shears
           g. Scissors
           h. Light fabric
           i. Varnishing lacquer – clear

Earlier cutouts have been made on coloured paper, or perhaps mounted on a coloured backing. Now we come to adding colour to the cutouts themselves.

The simplest way to add a contrasting colour is to cut shapes in a different colour and paste them down, either on top of or underneath the original cutout.

You can use pinking shears for a jagged or zigzag edge, a hole puncher to make small circles and ink or paint to draw on small details.

These make charming wall hangings, table mats, greetings cards and calendars, or may be used to beautify boxes and tins.

For a table mat, mount the cutout on hardboard with a good strong paste and cover with a light fabric. Alternatively, you could coat the top with a clear varnishing lacquer.

Arrange and mount a selection of cutouts, large and small, white-on-black, black-on-white and coloured, for an eye-catching wall hanging.

43

SILHOUETTES

HELPFUL HINTS

You can use any shape to make a silhouette, but profiles or side views are the most effective. Full facing figures can be used successfully if they demonstrate an activity such as jumping, skipping or dancing, when the arms and legs are spread out from the body. If the legs are not too close together and the arms are away from the body, figures walking or standing still can also be used.

Remember that the silhouette will face the opposite direction to the picture you have chosen when it is finished.

Look through old magazines, newspapers, comics and catalogues for figures and profiles of people and faces, animals, flowers, buildings and objects suitable for silhouettes. Try to imagine how they will look when they have been cut out. Be sure the shape is clear enough to show what it is when it is finished.

Keep several plastic bags handy to store suitable pictures for future use. Label the bags 'children', 'animals', 'flowers', and so on.

BASIC METHOD

Materials: a. Black poster paper
               b. Clean blotting paper or   e. Pictures
                    scrap paper   f. Scissors
               c. Newspaper   g. Stiff white card
               d. Paste and brush   or paper

When the picture you have chosen for your silhouette is printed on thin paper, use this method:

1.   Cut out the picture a little outside of its edges. Do not try to cut around its exact outline yet.

2.   Place the roughly cut picture with its face down on spread newspaper and brush paste evenly across the back.

3.   Lift the picture carefully and place it paste side down on the back of the black paper.

4.   If you are making more than one silhouette, place the pictures you are using closely together to avoid wasting the black paper.

5.   Put clean blotting or scrap paper over the picture. Press down and rub gently with your fingers to smooth the picture and soak up any extra paste.

6.   Place the black paper with its paste figure or figures under a piece of clean, dry paper on a flat surface. Then place a heavy weight such as books on top and allow the picture to dry.

7.   When the picture is completely dry, cut it out from the black sheet and lay the sheet aside to be used later for your next project.

8.   Before you begin the cut around the outline, be sure the picture is fully dry. The scissors will tear or pull the paper if it is slightly damp, so do not be tempted to start too soon.

9.   Cut from the right if you are right handed, and from the left if you are left handed, so that you can always see what you are doing.

10. Cut off the excess paper as you work, or it may get in the way of the scissors.

11. Turn the paper towards the scissors as you cut. At awkward corners or fine angles such as between lips or under the nose in profile, fingers, or on uneven edges of leaves, stop on an inward cut, then cut inward again from a little higher up to meet the first cut.

12. Taking special care with tricky corners will give a better result to the finished silhouette. Never pull at a piece of paper if it does not fall away immediately during cutting, as it may tear and spoil the outline or leave a fuzzy edge. Instead, make a slightly bigger cut from each direction until the unwanted piece does fall away.

13. The bottom edge of portraits may be cut in a straight line or a curve.

14. When you finish cutting, turn the picture over to the black side of the paper and there you have your silhouette. Lay it on white paper with the black side facing up and look to see whether any part needs trimming or a jagged edge cutting smooth.

15. When you are satisfied with the outline, place the silhouette on spread newspaper with the picture facing up. Brush paste evenly across the shape, then place it into position on a backing sheet of white paper or card.

16. Cover with clean blotting or scrap paper and gently smooth it down with your fingers. Do not bang it roughly with your fist, for the silhouette could move out of its position.

17. Remove the paper and cover the silhouette with clean, dry paper, place it under a weight and on a flat surface to dry.

TRICKIER CUTS

It is easier to tackle cutting away awkward and unwanted spaces before cutting around the rest of the outline, as the illustrations opposite show.

Cut the small space between the robin's legs first. Pierce the centre of the space with the point of a small pair of scissors.

Make cuts from the centre of the space to the edge of the outline, then cut around the inside edges of the legs.

Arrows indicate the spaces needing to be cut away before cutting around the main outline.

After cutting the final outline, fur, hair and grass can be indicated by making small, fine cuts on the edge of the silhouette. Cut first in one direction, then in the opposite direction. The cuts must be very fine for hair and fur, but grass may be a little coarser (see figs a and b).

To make the top of feathers, cut around the shape of the wing first. Make inward cuts in one direction following the wing tips. Then make new inward cuts in the opposite direction to meet the first cuts (see figs. c and d).

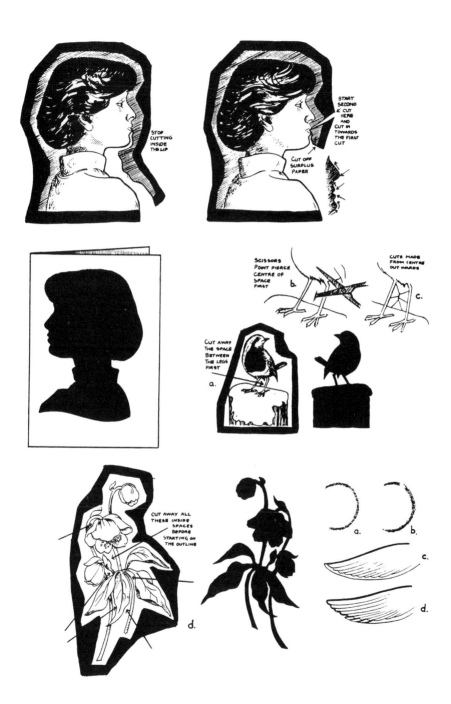

STOP CUTTING INSIDE THE LIP

START SECOND & CUT HERE AND CUT IN TOWARDS THE FIRST CUT

CUT OFF SURPLUS PAPER

SCISSORS POINT PIERCE CENTRE OF SPACE FIRST

b.

CUTS MADE FROM CENTRE OUTWARDS

c.

CUT AWAY THE SPACE BETWEEN THE LEGS FIRST

a.

CUT AWAY ALL THESE INSIDE SPACES BEFORE STARTING ON THE OUTLINE

d.

a.

b.

c.

d.

51

USING INDIAN INK 1

Materials   a. Black Indian ink or poster paint, and brush
                     b. Clean blotting or scrap paper
                     c. Newspaper
                     d. Paste and brush
                     e. Pictures
                     f. Scissors
                     g. Stiff white paper or card

When it is not possible to obtain black paper, silhouettes can be made with black Indian ink or, second best, black poster paint.

1. If the picture you have chosen is printed on stiff paper or card, such as a greetings card, just cut roughly around the picture. There is no need to paste it on to backing paper as then it would be more difficult to cut through the extra thickness.

2. Place the shape on spread newspaper with the picture facing down. Brush ink or paint all over the back, taking care to cover it completely.

3. When the ink is fully dry, turn the shape over to the picture side and cut carefully around the outline.

4. If you prefer, you can cut around the outline first and then ink over either the back or the front.

5. Paste the silhouette on to white paper or card. Soak up any extra paste by placing a piece of blotting or clean scrap paper over the top and gently smoothing down. Remove the blotting paper and cover the silhouette with clean, dry paper. Leave to dry on a flat surface under a heavy weight, such as books.

a.

b.

BLACK
POSTER P...

INDIAN INK

c.

USING INDIAN INK 2

Materials: a. Black Indian ink or poster paint, and brush
b. Clean blotting or scrap paper
c. Medium thick paper
d. Newspaper
e. Paste and brush
f. Pictures
g. Scissors
h. Stiff white paper or card

1. If the picture you have chosen is printed on thin paper, such as newsprint, cut the picture out roughly, and paste it on to paper of medium thickness with the picture facing up.

2. Cover the shape with a piece of clean, dry paper and leave to dry on a flat surface under a heavy weight, such as books.

3. When the picture is quite dry, place it on spread newspaper with the picture facing down. Brush ink or paint all over the back, taking care to cover it completely. Some types of paper may need a second coat when the first has dried. Do not brush too quickly or roughly, as small air bubbles could form and spoil your work.

4. After the ink or paint has dried completely, cut around the outline.

5. Paste the silhouette on to white paper or card. Soak up any extra paste by placing a piece of blotting or clean scrap paper over the top and gently smoothing down. Remove the blotting paper and cover the silhouette with clean, dry paper. Leave to dry on a flat surface under a weight.

You can ink over pictures printed on thin paper without backing them to sturdier paper, but there will be problems. Cut around the outline first in case the ink or paint soaks right through to the picture and prevents you from seeing its outline clearly. Thin paper will curl up under the brush and small pieces and edges may get in the way, making it very messy. Hold down the cut-out shape with a pencil or blade of scissors. Another possible hazard is that any printing on the picture might show through the ink or paint and spoil the silhouette.

BACKGROUND SCENERY

Materials: a. Cardboard
               b. Completed silhouettes
               c. Paste and brush

When you have mastered the cutouts and silhouettes already demonstrated, you may like to try more difficult variations.

The first illustration shows 2 pictures used to create a single silhouette. The man in old-fashioned clothing is cut from a magazine, pasted on to black paper and the silhouette cut out in the usual way. The village scene behind him is cut from another magazine and pasted on to cardboard backing. Its colours give an attractive background effect to the man's dark shape.

The ponies in the second illustration are cut from an old Christmas card and inked over the back. The background of a late evening scene comes from an old calendar and is mounted on stiff card.

These ideas make delightful small pictures to frame or use to make a new calendar.

COMPOSITE PICTURES

Materials: a. Black Indian ink or poster paint, and brush
                    b. Completed silhouettes
                    c. Paste and brush
                    d. Scraps of black paper
                    e. Stiff white card or paper

When you have mastered cutting silhouettes and discovered how easy it is to achieve attractive images, why not try making composite pictures? Design your own scenes by pasting 2, 3 or more silhouettes taken from different sources on to the same background.

In fig. a the castle and squirrel come originally from 2 different advertisements, the boy from an old birthday card and the trees are taken from the edges of a catalogue.

The boy in the tree in fig. b is taken from a clothing catalogue, the horse from a greetings card and the dog from a magazine. Fenceposts and grass are cut from scraps of black paper and the fence wire and hills are drawn in with black Indian ink or paint.

a.

b.

WHITE-ON-BLACK

Materials: a. Stiff black card or paper for backing
                  b. White paper for cutting

Rather than making silhouettes in black and mounting them on a white background, try the opposite approach. Cut outlines in white and paste on to a black backing sheet – these can be very attractive and the method is exactly the same as for the black-on-white silhouettes described on previous pages.

If you choose a picture on an old greetings card and the back of the sheet is white (and without any writing on it), you can cut around the outline straight away, as the card is usually stiff enough already. Paste it down, with the white side facing up, on a black background.

MULTI-SILHOUETTES

Materials: a. Board for cutting on – a chopping board, hardboard or thick, smooth cardboard
b. Clean blotting or scrap paper
c. Paper for cutting
d. Paste and brush
e. Pictures
f. Scissors
g. Sharp-pointed craft knife
h. White ink or paint, and brush

As your scissors must be able to cut through 4 layers for this design, it is essential to use a picture printed on thin paper and pasted on to thin black paper. Any simple shape is suitable – a flower head cut from a gardening catalogue is used in this example.

1.   Measure the shape and cut a square of black paper 4 times its size. Fold the square in half and in half again. Crease the folds firmly.

2.   Open the square out and paste the picture into one of the 4 small squares on the wrong side of the paper, taking care that the picture touches each of the 2 centre creases. Blot away any moisture or excess paste and allow to dry.

3.   Refold the square in half and half again with the picture on the top. Cut around the outline, leaving the parts which touch the folds intact so that it remains joined when opened out.

4.   For an added effect, use the point of a sharp knife to make small cuts in the centre, through all the thicknesses of paper. Rest the folded shape on a piece of board to do this, and take care not to cut yourself! Or, unfold the cutout and add several small dashes of white ink or paint instead.

a.

b.

CIRCULAR SILHOUETTES

Materials: a. Drawing compass, if available
              b. Paste and brush
              c. Paper for cutting
              d. Pencil
              e. Pictures
              f. Scissors
              g. Stiff white card or paper

A simple picture is ideal for a circular silhouette. Thin paper is essential, as you must cut through a number of paper thicknesses.

1.   Draw a circle with a drawing compass, or trace around a plate or other round object. Cut the circle out.

2.   Fold the shape in half, crease firmly and fold in half twice more, creasing each fold well.

3.   Open the circle out and paste the picture you have chosen into one of the 8 fold sections, on the wrong side of the paper. Part of the picture must touch the fold on both sides and the top edge. When dry, refold the circle as before, with the picture on the top.

4.   Cut out the top part first. Remember not to cut the folds where the picture touches them. Cut away the lower part and open out.

For a special occasion, mount the design on stiff card or paper and write a personal message or greeting in the centre.

a.

b.

65

DOUBLE SILHOUETTES

Materials: a. Black poster paper
             b. Paste and brush
             c. Pictures
             d. Scissors
             e. Stiff white card or paper

1. Find a suitable picture on thin paper, and cut out roughly.

2. Take a strip of black paper twice as long as the picture you have chosen. Paste the picture on to one end of the wrong side of the paper.

3. Fold the black paper in half, making sure that some part of the picture touches the fold. In the illustrations, the girl's hand is on the fold and the ground the fawn stands on is on the fold.

4. Hold the folded paper firmly and cut around the outline, through both thicknesses of paper. Cut first from the outside edges, then towards the fold, but do not cut out the picture where it touches the fold.

5. Open the silhouette and paste it carefully on to stiff white paper or card.

a.

b.

a.

b.

BUILDING UP SILHOUETTES

Pictures can be built up in the same way as described for making double silhouettes (see previous page).

The tree in the illustration is cut down its middle, then the straight edge pasted against the fold of the paper.

By extending the seat to join the tree trunk cutting, and cutting the ground between the boy's feet and the root of the tree in a continuous piece, these extra shapes could be included. When opened out, a double picture is formed.

a.

b.

ADDING DETAIL

Materials: a. Indian ink or poster paint, black and white, and brush
                       b. Silhouettes mounted on white card

A little artistry and imagination with black or white ink can enhance a quite simple silhouette when it has been mounted on card.

1. Draw water reeds in small groups and at different heights around the bird with ink. Add ripples of water around the clumps of reed and the bird's legs (see fig. a).

2. Again, draw clumps of reeds and water ripples around the swan (see fig. b).

3. Ink in water ripples and rocks around the fish.
   Use white paint to draw water across the fish itself (see fig. c).

4. Antennae, whiskers and other small features may be effectively inked in (see fig. d).

a.

b.

c.

d.

HIGHLIGHTING CUTS

Materials: a. Board for cutting on – a chopping board,
                     hardboard or thick, smooth cardboard
                  b. Craft knife with a sharp point
                  c. Paste and brush
                  d. Small, sharp scissors
                  e. Stiff white paper or card
                  f. Thin paper, black on one side

The skilful addition of certain cuts to a silhouette can bring the figure to life. Flowers are well suited to this. (See also the ballet dancers on page 77.)

Seed catalogues often picture lovely sprays of roses, lilies, tulips, daffodils and other flowers, singly rather than in bunches. Cut out with care and skill, these make stunning silhouettes.

1.   Paste the picture of a flower you have chosen on to the wrong side of the black paper. Allow to dry flat under a weight. Cut out the little pieces between stems, leaves and petals, then cut out around the outline.

2.   Lay the cutout on the cutting board with the picture facing upward. Decide which lines to cut to highlight the petals or veins in leaves and so on.

3.   Cut along the lines with a sharp knifepoint. Cut only along those lines you can clearly see. Remember not to make any cut so long that it severs that part completely from the rest of the figure.

4.   A slight cut has been made on the lily pictured to separate the petals, and some have a longer cut through their centres. Little curved pieces are nicked out of the stamens. Long cuts mark the centre of the leaves and short ones indicate where a stem or leaf crosses another.

CUTTING BOARD

Knife with
sharp
cutting point

73

INTRICATE CUTOUTS

Materials: a. Board for cutting on – a chopping board,
hardboard or thick, smooth cardboard
b. Craft knife with a sharp point
c. Paste and brush
d. Small sharp scissors
e. Stiff white paper or card
f. Thin black paper
g. Tracing paper
h. White ink or paint, and brush

The rose pictured is more intricate than usual in the cutting out
between leaves and stems. Make small cuts from the outline into
the edges of the petals, stopping before you meet another petal. Do
not cut every petal, just enough to highlight a few. Cut the centre
veins in the leaves before cutting the small ones – again, it is not
necessary to cut every single vein.

Hold the part you are cutting with the knife firmly with the fore
and middle finger – this leaves the other fingers free to move the
shape around when you cut a curved line.

To make the small veins, start cutting from the end first and
finish on the central vein. Cutting in the opposite direction could
cause the paper to tear.

Make long cuts in one sweeping movement rather than several
short ones, turning the paper towards the knife as you cut.

To broaden a cut to ensure it shows up on the black side, cut away
a thin shaving of paper very gently.

As you work, turn the silhouette over now and again to see how it
looks on the black side of the paper and whether any cuts need
more attention.

White paint and a fine brush may also be used to add lines to a
silhouette. First, make a tracing of the original picture, drawing in
the lines you want to transfer to the silhouette. Turn the tracing
over and draw over all the lines you see through the paper to
make them clearly visible. Use the tracing to show you where
white lines should be painted on to the silhouette. Do not make
lines too thick or heavy.

b.

OVERLAPPING FIGURES

Materials: a. Black poster paper
               b. Paste and brush   d. Small, sharp scissors
               c. Pictures   e. Stiff white card or paper

When looking for pictures to use for your silhouettes, you may find
one in which 2 heads lie together, one overlapping the other. When
cut out, one of the figures loses its identity and cannot be clearly
seen. Here's how to solve the problem:

1. Cut the figures out roughly and paste on to the wrong side on
   black paper in the way described on earlier pages. When dry,
   cut around the whole outline.
2. Now, very carefully cut around the outline of the head or
   figure which is on top or covering part of the lower figure, to
   separate it from its partner.
3. Paste down the top figure first on to white card or backing
   paper. Press down firmly, protecting the cutout by placing a
   piece of paper over it as you do so.
4. Slowly and carefully, ease the second figure back into its
   original position against the first figure, but leave a slight
   gap between the two. This should look like a fine, white line.
   Press down gently and allow to dry on a flat surface under a
   weight.

The ballet dancers pictured have extra cuts to highlight their
arms, but the cuts do not all extend as far as the edges of the
outline and are not separated from the rest of the figure –
otherwise you might end up with a jigsaw puzzle!

1. Cut around the outline as usual, after pasting the shape on
   to black paper. Then, carefully separate the ballerina from
   her partner with the scissors.
2. Make cuts along the arms of both figures, then cut away a very
   fine strip of paper to widen the cuts slightly. When pasted
   down, these narrow gaps will show up as a thin white line.
3. More care than ever is required when pasting the figures down.
   First, the ballerina is pasted down with her arm eased into
   position and then her partner is gently placed beside her.
   Press down firmly and dry on a flat surface under a weight.

These added touches make the silhouette a little more interesting.
It's not always necessary to make long cuts – a short one at the
bottom of a jacket, along a lapel or around a ribbon may provide
all the impact the silhouette needs.

a.

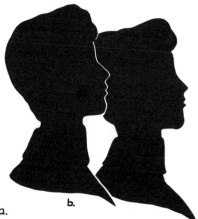

b.

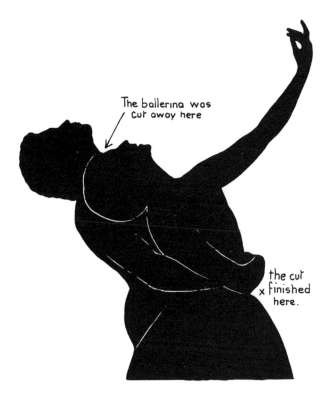

The ballerina was cut away here

the cut
x finished
here.

HALF-PROFILES

Materials   a. Black poster paper
                    b. Board for cutting on – a chopping board,
                        piece of hardboard or thick, smooth cardboard
                    c. Paste and brush
                    d. Pencil
                    e. Pictures
                    f. Scissors
                    g. Sharp craft knife
                    h. Steel ruler
                    i. Stiff white card or paper

You may wish to use a picture which only shows half a profile instead of the whole head.

1. With a ruler and pencil, draw a border around the figure before cutting the shape out roughly.

2. Paste the shape on to the wrong side of black paper. When quite dry, place on a piece of board and cut along the border on the inside and outside using a sharp knife and steel ruler. Cut the profile outline with scissors.

Pasted on to card, this makes an attractive study.

a.

b.

79

PORTRAITS

Materials: a. Black Indian ink or poster paint, and brush
                b. Black poster paper with a white back is excellent
                c. Board to work on
                d. Good tracing paper
                e. Scissors
                f. Sticky tape
                g. Well-sharpened pencil
                   (no harder than B or you could mark the photograph)
                h. White paper

It is possible to do portraits of members of the family or friends provided you have a good clear photograph taken in profile. Snapshots may be too small, but a studio portrait or another larger photograph with a clear profile is ideal.

1. If you cannot obtain the poster paper with a white backing, cut a piece of white paper a little larger than the photograph you are using. Paint one side of the paper with ink or paint. If necessary, apply a second coat after the first has dried.

2. Cut a piece of tracing paper, slightly larger than the photograph, to allow it to cover the front and fold over the photograph's back. Secure the paper firmly to your working board with sticky tape across each corner to prevent it moving.

3. With a pencil, draw very softly but firmly around the photograph's outline – the head, neck and shoulders.

4. Remove the sticky tape, lift the tracing paper off the photograph and place pencil-side down on the white side of the black paper (be sure the ink has dried first). Again, fasten both to the board with sticky tape. Gently, but firmly, using the back of a scissor's handle or your thumb nail, rub all over the pencilled lines on the tracing paper. This will transfer the tracing to the white surface, so be careful to rub over every part.

5. Remove the sticky tape and tracing paper. Notice the figure outline on the white surface faces the opposite direction to the original photograph. Cut around the outline. Finish off the bottom of the figure with a slight curve.

6. Brush paste all over the white side of the paper and stick down to white backing paper or card and dry under a weight on a flat surface.

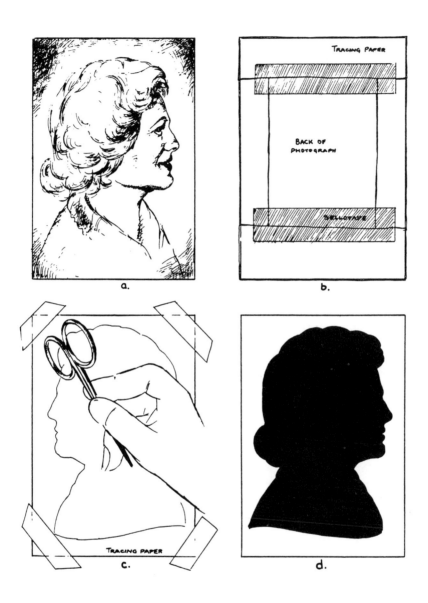

a.

TRACING PAPER

BACK OF PHOTOGRAPH

SELLOTAPE

b.

TRACING PAPER

c.

d.

LIFE-SIZED SILHOUETTES

Materials: a. Black Indian ink or paint, and brush if necessary
                b. Black poster paper, if available
                c. Drawing pins or blue tack
                d. Electric lamp   e. Scissors
                f. Soft, well-sharpened pencil   g. Stiff white paper
                h. White pencil, crayon or chalk if necessary

In earlier times, when silhouettes were very fashionable, the artist did not have photographs available from which to make tracings. Instead, the artist sat the person to be drawn on a chair in front of a paper screen. A light placed a little distance away threw the sitter's shadow on to the screen. Sitting on the other side of the screen, the artist drew around the outline of the shadow on his side of the paper.

Later, the artist was able to use a pantograph greatly to reduce the size of the head, giving a miniature portrait in black.

Full-sized portraits make lovely silhouettes and can be very eye-catching when framed.

1. If black poster paper with a white back is available, this is best. Otherwise, use stiff white paper and paint one side black with ink or paint either before or after making the cutout. You could use paper which is black on both sides, but then you would need to use a white pencil, crayon or chalk sharpened to a fine point for your drawing.

2. Fix the sheet of paper, white side facing out, to a flat vertical surface – a door or wall – with drawing pins or blue tack, at the height of the person's head to be drawn. Protect the surface first with another clean sheet of paper in case the black surface leaves marks.

3. Have the subject stand as flat as possible against the wall with either their back or front against it – not standing sideways. Have them turn their head sideways against the paper with their chin up and mouth slightly open.

4. Arrange an electric lamp a little distance away (not too near!), level with the head, to throw the shadow of the head on to the paper. With a soft, well-sharpened pencil, draw around the outline of the shadow.

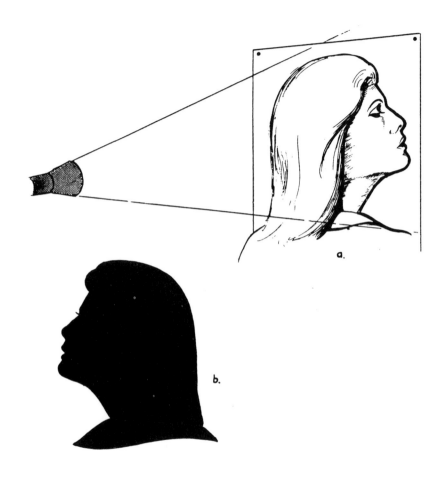

a.

b.

---

5. Remove the paper from the wall, replace with another sheet and stand against the wall yourself in the same way while your friend draws around your shadow.

6. Then you can cut out your own silhouettes and paste them on to a white background.

This makes an enjoyable and unusual party activity. When everyone's silhouette is finished and pinned up, it's fun to guess who's who.

REDUCING

Materials: a. Black Indian ink or poster paint, and brush
                b. Board to work on
                c. Pencil
                d. Rubber
                e. Ruler
                f. Sticky tape
                g. White paper

1. Measure the silhouette background and mark it off to form squares. When ruling lines across the white background, use a soft, light pencil so that the lines may be rubbed out afterwards. Do not rule lines across the silhouette. Number each line across the top, bottom and down both sides (see fig. a).

2. After deciding what size you want your small silhouette to be, take another piece of paper, measure and rule the same number of lines to form the grid, in a smaller size of squares. Number the lines across the top, bottom and down both sides in the same way you numbered the lines on the original (see fig. b).

3. Copy the outline of the silhouette by marking the smaller squares where they correspond with the larger squares on the silhouette, keeping to the same numbered lines for each step. Check often to make sure you are on the correct line or square (see fig. c).

4. It may help to secure the small grid to a drawing board to prevent it moving. Use one hand to draw and the other to move slowly from line to line. Do not rush, for one false move will spoil your outline (see fig. d).

5. When finished, and you are satisfied that the outline looks just like the larger silhouette in miniature, carefully paint in the shape with black Indian ink or paint.

6. Gently rub out the pencilled grid on the original silhouette and the smaller one when the ink has completely dried (see fig. e).

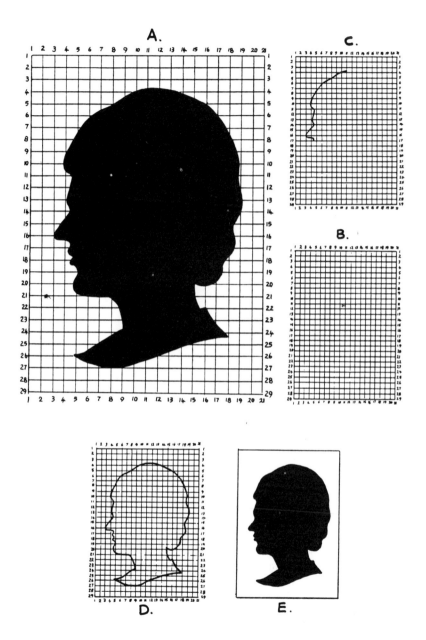

A.

C.

B.

D.

E.

ENLARGING

Materials: a. Black Indian ink or poster paint, and brush
                b. Board to work on
                c. Pencil
                d. Rubber
                e. Ruler
                f. Sticky tape
                g. Tracing paper – if necessary
                h. White paper
                i. White ink or paint, and brush – if necessary

To enlarge any small picture, the method described on the previous page is used in reverse.

Remember that if you are reducing or enlarging any picture other than a silhouette, the grid lines must be ruled right across the picture to enable you to draw in the extra details as well as the outline. If you would prefer not to rule lines across the drawings to be copied, cover with good clear tracing paper, secure with sticky tape, and lightly draw the grid pattern on this.

1.   Measure the small picture and rule it off into squares. Number each line across the top, bottom and down both sides.

2.   On a larger sheet of paper, measure and rule off exactly the same number of lines in a larger size of squares. Number the lines in the same way as for the small picture.

3.   Step by step, carefully copy the outline of the small picture on to the larger grid, keeping to the corresponding line or square. Check closely when finished, before inking or painting the shape. In a drawing other than a silhouette, add any details in the same way. One false line will spoil your outline, so be sure to check it often and do not rush your work.

4.   After inking or painting the shape, wait until it has completely dried before gently rubbing out the pencil lines of the grid. Rub out the lines on the original, small picture too.

If you think it would help you to draw the grid lines across the black of the silhouette, use a soft white pencil or well-sharpened chalk which can be easily erased afterwards.

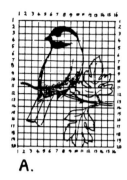

A.

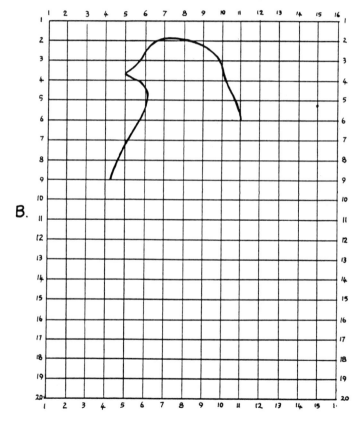

B.

USING A PANTOGRAPH

It is possible to reduce or enlarge silhouettes and pictures using a mechanical method rather than 'squaring up' with a grid. This is done with the aid of a pantograph, which can be obtained from art shops. Instructions for its use are given with it, or you can make it if you are skillful enough!

These illustrations show the use of a pantograph to enlarge 2 drawings, the first to 3 times its original size and the second to twice its original size.

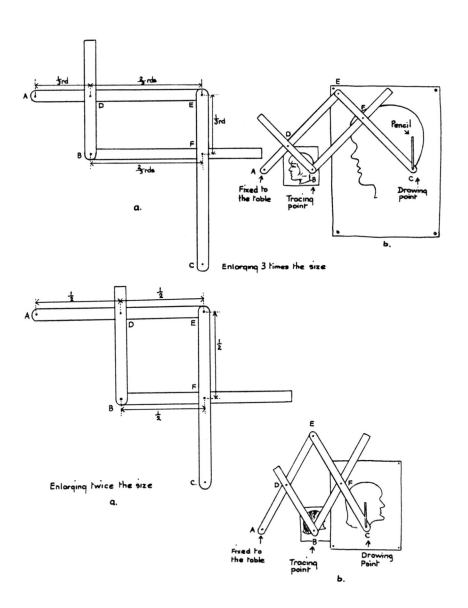

A

⅓rd   ⅔rds

D   E

⅓rd

B

F

⅔rds

a.

c.   Enlarging 3 times the size

E

F

Pencil

D

A
Fixed to
the table   B   C
Tracing   Drawing
point   point

b.

A

½   ½

D   E

½

F

B   ½

C.

Enlarging twice the size

a.

E

D   F

A
Fixed to
the table   B   C
Tracing   Drawing
point   Point

b.

89

IDEAS FOR YOUR SILHOUETTES

The possible uses for your silhouette cutouts are unlimited.

a. Two observation games, one in black-on-white and the other reversed, in white-on-black.

b. A poster to advertise a coming event.

c. A decorative lid for a plastic or other container.

d. A small, framed portrait for dresser or shelves.

e. An appealing programme cover.

f. Greetings cards for special friends.

g. A calendar.

h. Matchbox covers and lids for other boxes.

i. Gift tags.

A GALLANTY SHOW

Materials: a. Black cartridge paper or thin card
                 b. Black Indian ink or poster paint, and brush
                 c. Needle and cotton
                 d. Old magazines, scenic calendars, catalogues, etc.
                 e. Paste and brush
                 f. Scissors
                 g. Two-pronged paper clips

A gallanty show is a pantomime of moving shadows. These were very popular in days gone by and rivalled Punch and Judy shows. You can use the silhouettes of figures and scenery you make to create a show of your own. See the instructions on page 94 for making a screen and follow the steps described here to make the characters.

Scenery and Figures: From magazines, catalogues, calendars, etc. cut out pictures of figures and objects you want for your show (or draw them yourself, if you prefer to do so). Paste all of them on to the white side of the stiff cartridge paper or card as described earlier in silhouette cutting, but leave an extra long strip at the foot of each piece that is to be moved (see fig. A). After cutting out, ink or paint the other, picture side, in black too. If you do not have black paper or card, follow the same procedure with white paper or card, then ink or paint both sides of the cutout black.

It is fun to make parts of figures and animals move (see fig. B). After cutting out the figure, cut off the limb, tail or part you wish to make mobile where it joins the body (a), paste it on to black paper and recut it out with a little extra length at the top. Thread a length of cotton through the top and reattach the part to the body with a two-pronged paper clip (b). When gently pulled, that part will move. Birds in flight, stars, moon, etc. can be fastened to cotton and hung from the top of the screen (c).

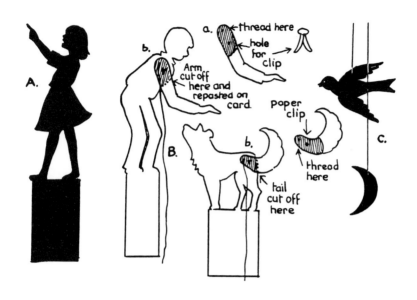

A.

b.
a. ← thread here
hole
for
clip

Arm
cut off
here and
repasted on
card

paper
clip

B.

b.
thread
here

tail
cut off
here

C.

A SIMPLE SCREEN

Materials: a. Black Indian ink or poster paint, and brush
               b. Coloured pictures for scenery
               c. Elastic or tape
               d. Electric lamp (100 watt) or strong torch
               e. Large cardboard carton f. Paper clips
               g. Paste and brush   h. Pencil
               i. Ruler   j. Scissors
               k. Sellotape   l. Stapler
               m. Tracing paper   n. White chalk

1.   With the carton, the largest you can obtain, cut away the top, bottom and one side. In the centre section, rule and cut a large hole for the screen. Securely paste an uncreased sheet of tracing paper over this hole for the screen. Cover the edges of the paper with sellotape to prevent them coming unstuck and curling up. Make very sure the paper is really taut (see fig. a).

2.   Paint the other side of the carton (which will face the audience) black (fig. b).

3.   Use a stapler to fasten 2 lengths of elastic or tape to the foot of the screen. Have one almost level with the bottom edge of the screen hole and the other 20mm (.75") lower (fig. c). These are to slip the stationary scenery or movable figures and small scenery into when performing. The scenery can be one large piece which covers the entire screen, or smaller, movable pieces. To make the large scenery, mark the centre of the black paper or card to which you have pasted the picture scene and the outline of the screen hole with chalk, then cut out the scenery so that the edges of it are INSIDE those lines (fig. d). Keep it in place at the top of the framework with paper clips, and slip the bottom into BOTH lengths of elastic or tape, to keep it steady. Fig. (e) shows small background items and figures in position.

4.   Place the light above your head and behind you to shine on the screen. Do remember to keep your head and hands about level or lower than the bottom of the screen (see fig. f).

5.   Have someone tell the story while you move the figures. Hold each figure close to the screen, and if one has to be left 'on stage' while you bring up another, remember to slip it under the bottom elastic first, before bringing it into view.

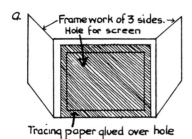

a. Framework of 3 sides. →
Hole for screen

Tracing paper glued over hole

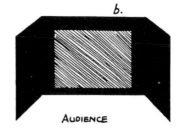

b.

AUDIENCE

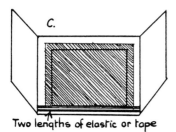

c.

Two lengths of elastic or tape

Paper clips d.

large scenery kept firmly in place. Dotted lines - the screen hole.

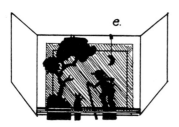

e.

Small item of scenery and movable figure.

f.

If you have enjoyed making these paper cuts and silhouettes,
you will enjoy Rosalie Brown's other handcraft books.
For a complete list of those and Jade Publishers' other handcraft
books, please write to:

Dept EP
Jade Publishers
15 Stoatley Rise
Haslemere
Surrey GU27 1AF